JESUS PRESENTED AT THE TEMPLE

MATTHEW 2:1-12

THE MAGI BRING GIFTS

LUKE 2:1-20

MATTHEW 2:13-18

THE FAMILY FLEES
TO EGYPT

MATTHEW 2:19-23

THE RETURN TO NAZARETH

In memory of my in-laws, Harold and Betty Williamson, who were full of faith,
determination, and love. Your legacy will continue for generations to come.

—*D.W.*

*   *   *

For Eugennie, Patrice, Tonii-Ann, and Camryn,
you are the stars that help light my life.

—*R.E.*

BROWN BABY JESUS

All Scripture quotations are taken from the Holy Bible, New International Version®, NIV®. Copyright © 1973, 1978, 1984, 2011 by Biblica Inc.™ Used by permission of Zondervan. All rights reserved worldwide. (www.zondervan.com). The "NIV" and "New International Version" are trademarks registered in the United States Patent and Trademark Office by Biblica Inc.™

Text copyright © 2022 by Dorena Williamson
Cover art and interior illustrations copyright © 2022 by Ronique Ellis

All rights reserved.

Published in the United States by WaterBrook, an imprint of Random House, a division of Penguin Random House LLC.

WATERBROOK® and its deer colophon are registered trademarks of Penguin Random House LLC.

ISBN 978-0-593-23638-3
Ebook ISBN 978-0-593-23639-0

The Library of Congress catalog record is available at https://lccn.loc.gov/2021035836.

Printed in the United States of America

waterbrookmultnomah.com

10 9 8 7 6 5 4 3 2 1

First Edition

Book and cover design by Annalisa Sheldahl

SPECIAL SALES Most WaterBrook books are available at special quantity discounts when purchased in bulk by corporations, organizations, and special-interest groups. Custom imprinting or excerpting can also be done to fit special needs. For information, please email specialmarketscms@penguinrandomhouse.com.

Brown Baby Jesus

written by
Dorena Williamson

WATERBROOK

illustrated by
Ronique Ellis

Mary and Joseph made their way through the Egyptian marketplace with their brown baby Jesus in tow.

Jesus's eyes took in the traders from near and far.
His little nose filled with the scents of fruit, bread, and spices.
His face lit up at the sight of children threading colorful clay beads.

SING TO GOD, YOU KINGDOMS OF THE EARTH, SING PRAISE TO THE LORD.
—PSALM 68:32

Just weeks before, Magi from the east had visited the family in Bethlehem, bringing gold, frankincense, and myrrh to honor Jesus as the **king of the Jews.**

After the Magi left, an angel warned Joseph
in a dream that King Herod was angry about
their visit and wanted to kill Jesus.

While the family fled to Egypt, jealous Herod sent his soldiers
to kill all the baby boys two years and younger.

"Look, Abba. Soldier!" Jesus exclaimed.

Seeing the soldiers reminded Joseph
of the angel's warning.

NATIONS WILL COME TO YOUR LIGHT, AND KINGS TO THE BRIGHTNESS OF YOUR DAWN. —ISAIAH 60:3

Mary thought about when they took Jesus to the temple.
A man named Simeon said that Jesus would reveal **God's light**
to people all over the world, but he also said that Mary's heart
would feel sorrow because some would want to hurt Jesus.

Resting her chin on His bushy hair, Mary held
her son close and prayed for God's peace.

As the family walked beside the Nile River, Mary and Joseph were reminded of another baby boy.

IN YOUR UNFAILING LOVE YOU WILL LEAD THE PEOPLE YOU HAVE REDEEMED.
—EXODUS 15:13

Long ago, the great leader Moses had been placed in this river to protect him from another angry ruler. Moses's little basket bobbed along until it floated right by the princess of Egypt, who raised him as her son.

When Moses grew up, God used him to deliver the Israelites out of Egypt and lead them to the Promised Land.

"One day You, too, will be a deliverer," Joseph spoke over Jesus as they watched a trade ship disappear from view.

SHE WILL GIVE BIRTH TO A SON, AND YOU ARE TO GIVE HIM THE NAME JESUS, BECAUSE HE WILL SAVE HIS PEOPLE FROM THEIR SINS.

—MATTHEW 1:21

As Mary spun wool into yarn, she thought about the words Joseph had spoken. She knew that God had mapped out a special story for her son that spanned many generations and even included different nations.

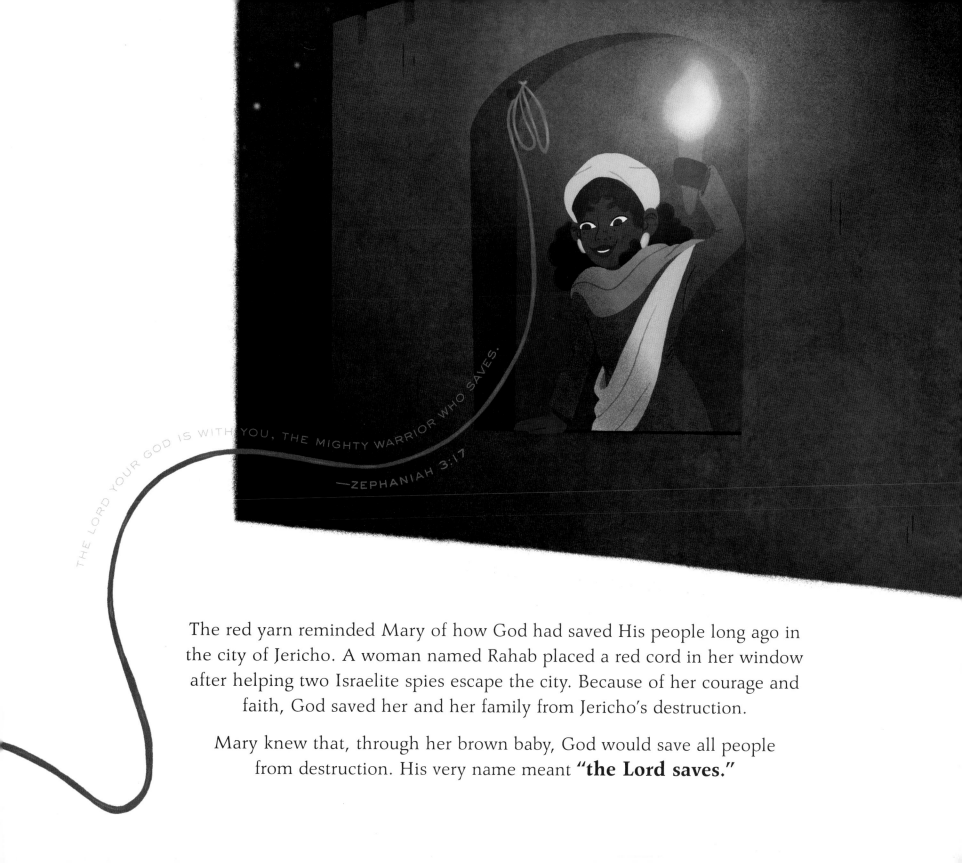

THE LORD YOUR GOD IS WITH YOU, THE MIGHTY WARRIOR WHO SAVES.

—ZEPHANIAH 3:17

The red yarn reminded Mary of how God had saved His people long ago in the city of Jericho. A woman named Rahab placed a red cord in her window after helping two Israelite spies escape the city. Because of her courage and faith, God saved her and her family from Jericho's destruction.

Mary knew that, through her brown baby, God would save all people from destruction. His very name meant **"the Lord saves."**

As she made bread, Mary thought about the widow Ruth. Ruth had picked up leftover grain so she and her mother-in-law, Naomi, would have something to eat.

Although Ruth was from a foreign land, God gave her a place among His people when she married Boaz, and she became the great-grandmother of King David.

David married Bathsheba, a widow who God comforted with the birth of a son named Solomon. When he grew up, Solomon built the temple, a special place of worship for God's people.

God kept showing up for His people, replacing death and sorrow with life and **joy**. Then He made His home with humankind when Jesus **entered the world** wrapped in the brown skin of a newborn baby.

His coming was good news of great joy for all people. Mary smiled, knowing that her son would be a greater king than His ancestor David and that He would **reign forever**.

Mary understood that God had shown mercy from generation to generation.

She knew that mercy had been poured out for a widow named Tamar,
who was mistreated and alone until God blessed her with two sons.

She had seen mercy flow to her cousin Elizabeth, who was
given a miracle son in her old age.

She had felt God's mercy in Anna, an elderly woman at the temple who was so excited to meet newborn Jesus, God's promised deliverer.

And as Mary looked at her brown baby, she saw in Him
God's promise of mercy for all people.

ONE GENERATION COMMENDS YOUR WORKS TO ANOTHER;
THEY TELL OF YOUR MIGHTY ACTS. —PSALM 145:4

Like a weaver using colorful threads that make a beautiful cloth,
God had designed quite a story for Mary's brown baby Jesus.

THE WORD BECAME FLESH AND MADE HIS DWELLING AMONG US. WE HAVE SEEN HIS GLORY, THE GLORY OF THE ONE AND ONLY SON.

An **uncommon** story that included royals. A **welcoming** story that included foreigners. A **loving** story that included heartbroken widows. And a **magnificent** story that included humble people like Mary and Joseph.

As the sun set and the moon rose in the African sky,
Mary watched her brown baby Jesus climb into Joseph's arms.

"Story, Eema?" He asked, gazing at her with expectation.

Thinking of all she had held in her heart throughout the day,
Mary knew the perfect story to tell. Her heart rejoiced as she
began to tell her son about His earthly family.

"In the beginning, God took soil from the ground and made Adam and Eve in His very image," she began.

"Later, a man named Noah found favor with God and was saved from the Flood. God told Noah's three sons, Shem, Ham, and Japheth, to be fruitful and fill the earth—and that's what they did! Many nations formed and spread far and wide."

THEIR APPOINTED TIMES IN HISTORY AND THE BOUNDARIES OF THEIR LANDS.

AND HE MARKED OUT

HOULD INHABIT THE WHOLE EARTH;

—ACTS 17:26

"From Shem came Your ancestors like Abraham, Judah, and David," Joseph said, picking up where Mary had left off. "And from Ham came Your ancestors Tamar, Rahab, and Bathsheba. These two lines blended together, and their blood runs through You."

"Your woolly hair and bronze skin are a beautiful part of how God made You and who You come from," Mary added.

ABRAHAM

TAMAR

JUDAH

RAHAB

BATHSHEBA

DAVID

I PRAISE YOU BECAUSE I AM FEARFULLY AND WONDERFULLY MADE. —PSALM 139:14

"God promised our ancestors Abraham and Sarah that every family on the earth would be blessed through them. And God kept His promise through the generations that led to me, Eema, and now You!" Joseph said, finishing the story.

Then Mary sang a psalm over their brown baby boy.

WHOEVER DWELLS IN THE SHELTER OF THE MOST HIGH WILL REST IN THE SHADOW OF THE ALMIGHTY. I WILL SAY OF THE LORD, "HE IS MY REFUGE AND MY FORTRESS, MY GOD, IN WHOM I TRUST." —PSALM 91:1-2

The family stayed in Egypt for many years, until one night an angel told Joseph that it was safe for the family to return to Israel.

"We're going home, son," Joseph said as they began their journey.

WHEN ISRAEL WAS A CHILD, I LOVED HIM, AND OUT OF EGYPT I CALLED MY SON. —HOSEA 11:1

And in Nazareth, Jesus continued to grow,
full of wisdom and grace.

GENESIS 38

JUDAH & TAMAR

GENESIS 12:2-3, GENESIS 18:1-13

ABRAHAM & SARAH

GENESIS 6:9-10, GENESIS 9:1, GENESIS 10:32

NOAH & HIS SONS

JOSEPH

GENESIS 2:4-25

ADAM & EVE

BROW
BA

JESUS'S
FAMILY TREE